MW01487577

SUGAR IN OUR WOUNDS

BY
DONJA R. LOVE

★

★

DRAMATISTS
PLAY SERVICE
INC.

NOTE ON BILLING

SPECIAL NOTE ON SONGS/RECORDINGS

SUGAR IN OUR WOUNDS was originally produced by the Manhattan Theatre Club (Lynne Meadow, Artistic Director; Barry Grove, Executive Producer) on June 18, 2018. It was directed by Saheem Ali. The set design was by Arnulfo Maldonado, the costume design was by Dede Ayite, the lighting design was by Jason Lyons, the sound design was by Palmer Hefferan, the original music was by Michael Thurber, the production stage manager was Jereme Kyle Lewis, and the stage manager was Erin McCoy. The cast was as follows:

JAMES	Sheldon Best
HENRY	Chinaza Uche
AUNT MAMA	Stephanie Berry
MATTIE	Tiffany Rachelle Stewart
ISABEL	Fern Cozine

SUGAR IN OUR WOUNDS was developed by The Playwrights Realm (Katherine Kovner, Artistic Director; Roberta Pereira, Producing Director).

CHARACTERS

JAMES
M, late teens, Black; he's young, precocious, and innocent—according to his heart; but let the world tell you, he's a man. He has a magical relationship with a tall, tall tree.

HENRY
M, late teens/early twenties, Black; he's tall, strong, and harder than the world that made him this way; and he's dark—real dark. His skin looks like the midnight hour—like something people pray to. He has an incredible tenderness that he doesn't let anyone see, that he desperately wants someone to see.

AUNT MAMA
W, there's no age here—that's for a reason, Black; she's an old, old magic woman who's probably older than God—let her tell it. She has a gentleness to her that can be hard to see thanks to her quick tongue.

MATTIE
W, early twenties, Black; she's a girl who just wants to be loved. Despite the scars on her face, she is very pretty. She has skin so yellow it makes the sun jealous.

ISABEL
W, early twenties, White; she has a desire for things she shouldn't touch, and it's dangerous—at least for those she tries to touch. But with that, she's as well intentioned as she possibly could be—for a white girl.

TIME

Summer
1862

PLACE

Somewhere down South
By a tall, tall tree

ABOUT THE SKIN

The actor playing Henry *must* have skin as dark as a starless midnight. The actress playing Mattie *must* have skin so light it could make the sun jealous. The actors playing James and Aunt Mama should have skin tones that exist somewhere between the actors playing Henry and Mattie.

NOTE

This play is part 1 of a trilogy that explores Queer love through Black History (slavery, the Civil Rights movement, the Black Lives Matter movement). Part 2 is FIREFLIES.

If desired, the playwright gives permission for an intermission to happen after Scene Five.

"When the wounds right he run down get some sugar

Prolly pour it on so it sting not as bad as salt, but it get sticky
Melt in the singing Southern sun.

Sweetness draw all the bugs and infection to the sores… Sweetness
harder to wash.

It become molasses in all that heat and blood…"

—*Marcus; or The Secret of Sweet*
Tarell Alvin McCraney

SUGAR IN OUR WOUNDS

Scene 1

Dark.

We hear...

Humming.

Humming in the air.

It makes the whole air sweet.

It's wind.

But not just any kind of wind—talking wind.

It says, "James."

We see...

Stars kiss the midnight sky.

And,

A tree.

It's big.
Real.
Big.

Some say it go straight up to heaven.
Its branches spread out like wings.

It beats.

Beats.
Beats.

Like a heart.

In an open space there stands a boy.

James.

He's young, and innocent—according to his heart; but let the world tell you, he's a man.

He stares up at the tree.
He's mystified by it.

No one would be surprised if he were here, standing in this exact spot, staring at it for hours.

He begins to weep.
He wipes tears from his eyes.

Then…

An old, old woman comes up behind him. She takes her time. That's all she know to do…

Take time.

It's Aunt Mama.

She's probably older than God, let her tell it.

JAMES. Aunt Mama.
Remind me 'bout this tree uhgain.

AUNT MAMA. You always been uh learnin' boy.

JAMES. Please.
Remind me.
Why it's so big?

AUNT MAMA. It's blood at dat root.
Help it grow.
Help make it strong.
Look at dem branches—day bodies.
Da blood come from some strong menz.

JAMES. Like ma daddy?

AUNT MAMA. Yes'um.
Ya daddy was hunged on dis here tree.
And his daddy.
And his daddy 'fore dat.
And his.
All da ways up ta Jesus,
bein' hunged on da cross.

Dat's why it so tall.
It go straights up ta heaven.
If ya quiets nuff ya can hear 'em.

> *He/we hear(s)…*
> *"Jaaaaaaaames."*

JAMES. I hear 'em.
They callin' ma name.

AUNT MAMA. Really?

JAMES. Yes.

> *Beat.*

AUNT MAMA. It's gonna end wit chu.
You got somefin' betta den strong.
You got smarts.
You gots uh sweetness ta ya dat make ya special.

> *The stars continue to kiss the sky's dark skin, as it wraps itself around the heavenbound tree.*
>
> *They stare.*
>
> *And listen to the wind.*
>
> *Hum.*

Scene 2

Early night.

We're in a shack. It's small, old, and dirty.

There are three objects that one can only gather are beds? Maybe? A table. A big wooden block, for sitting. Two metal buckets, one for drinking; the other for…the bathroom.

And a chair.
A very nice chair.
It actually looks like it doesn't belong here.

James sits in THAT chair.

He's reading a newspaper—very quickly. He turns a page before the previously read page touches the old page.

He reads.
And reads.
And reads.

At this exact moment, he's good.

Then…

He stops.
He listens. Intently.

He gets up and looks out the window. He runs back over to the chair. He grabs the newspaper and hides it.

ANYWHERE.

Don't think too hard on it.
Just hide it.

He goes back over to the chair and dusts it off.

Then…

He sits on the wooden block. The shack's door opens.

In walks Isabel, a white woman, 20ish; she's strikingly beautiful—and knows it. At her core, she's as well intentioned as she possibly could be—for a white woman.

ISABEL. James.

  James stands.

JAMES. Hello, Miss Isabel.

ISABEL. You ready?

JAMES. Yes, Miss Isabel.

  Isabel walks in and goes straight to the chair.
  She sits.
  She's comfortable. Clearly this is her chair.

ISABEL. What's that smell?

  James runs over to the metal bucket. He takes it outside and
  dumps it out. He comes back in—metal bucket in hand.

Leave that thing outside.
I don't know why y'all keep it in here.
Don't make a lick of sense.

JAMES. Sorry ma'am.

> *James takes the bucket back outside.*
> *He reenters.*

ISABEL. Now, come on, sit on down here.

> *James sits. Next to Isabel.*

I bet you've been waiting for this all day. Haven't you?

> *James nods.*

I know.

> *Isabel pulls something from out her bag.*
> *It's a book: the Bible.*
> *She hands it to James.*

Now, I can't stay too long.
It's funky up in here.
And this Summer sun don't help it none.

> *She fans herself.*
> *The heat combined with the stench has her a bit annoyed.*

Let's pick up where we left off yesterday.
Go on.
Read.

> *James begins to read.*
> *He's really good.*

JAMES. "…The king arose very early in the morning, and went in haste unto the den of lions. And when he came to the den, he cried with a la-men-ta-ble? Lamentable."

ISABEL. Yes. Lamentable.

JAMES. What does lamentable mean, ma'am?

ISABEL. Lamentable means: to be mournful, to grieve.

JAMES. Oh. "…He cried with a lamentable voice unto Daniel: and the king spake and said to Daniel, 'O Daniel, servant of the living God, is thy God, whom thou servest continually, able to deliver thee from the lions?' Then said Daniel unto the king, 'O king, live forever. My God hath sent His angel, and hath shut the lions' mouths, that they have not hurt me: forasmuch as before him, in… no…in…no…in—'"

ISABEL. Here. Let me see. Let's sound it out.

James hands Isabel the Bible.

JAMES and ISABEL. In-no-cen-cy.
In-no-cen-cy.

ISABEL. That's it.
Now go on.

JAMES. "Innocency was found in me..." Ma'am, what does innocency mean?

ISABEL. Innocency means: to be pure, to be of virtue.

JAMES. Oh. "Innocency was found in me; and also before thee, O king, have I done no hurt." So Daniel wasn't killed by all those lions, ma'am?

ISABEL. Not a single scratch.

JAMES. So the king tried to abuse his power by harming Daniel, but Daniel came out on top, ma'am?

ISABEL. Correct.

JAMES. *(Genuine.)* Was Daniel Black, ma'am?

A moment.

ISABEL. Don't be foolish, James. And don't ask me any more questions. Okay? You slowing down your learning now. Just read.

JAMES. "The king was *(Needing help with this word, but too scared to ask for it.)* ex-ceed-ing-ly glad for him, and commanded that they should take Daniel up out of the den. So Daniel was taken up out of the den, and no manner of hurt was found upon him, because he believed in his God. And the king commanded, and they brought those men which had accused Daniel, and they cast them into the den of lions, them, their children, and their wives; and the lions had the mastery of them, and brake all their bones in pieces or ever they came at the bottom of the den. Then king Darius wrote unto all people, nations, and languages, that dwell in all the earth: Peace be multiplied unto you."

ISABEL. Wonderful.
Simply wonderful.
You blow me away.
Every.

Single.

Time.

You read so well, James!

So very well.

What did you get from that reading?

JAMES. That Daniel's faith in God is what saved him, ma'am.

ISABEL. Yes, and what else?

He thinks.

JAMES. *(Nervous.)* Uh, that Daniel was not Black, ma'am?

ISABEL. That he was not. And, also, what you failed to see is that passage was an analogy for what's going on right now. Us Southerners are Daniel, and the lions are the Yankees. No matter how much they try, we will come out on top because we're doing the work of the Lord down here.

A moment.

JAMES. Should I continue reading, ma'am?

ISABEL. No. We're done for this session. I have to go and write my William. Now he really is doing the work of the Lord by fighting so you can keep this good life. Plus, this smell gonna be the death of me.

James gives Isabel back her book.

I swear, they need to have you in a museum. You read so well. Ever since I caught you reading one of my letters, you got much better since I started learning you. I'm proud of myself. If I can teach a nigger I know for sure I can teach a regular person.

Silence.

Say "thank you." When someone gives you a compliment you say "thank you." That's polite.

JAMES. Thank you, ma'am.

ISABEL. You so well trained.

You sweet.

Real.

Sweet.

James awkwardly smiles.

I like ones like you.

Isabel puts her hand on James' knee.
Then…
She rubs his leg.

You like ones like me?

James doesn't say a word.
He tries to open his mouth.
But nothing comes out.

Only fear.

So…
He smiles.
Beat.

Now don't go filling that inquisitive head of yours. You *nowhere* near my type, boy. You too…skinny. I like 'em big. Like my William. And I'm just here to teach you, to help, silly. I really do want the best for you… Plus, this give me something to do while my William is away.

Beat.

And remember, don't you tell a soul about any of this…if you do, you'll end up being the one letting out a lamentable cry.

She smiles.

James smiles too—because he must.

Then…

The door swings open.

It's Aunt Mama.

Followed by Mattie. A young woman who looks like ~~she's had better~~, she's had days. Despite the scars on her face, she's a very pretty girl. She's 20ish—with skin so yellow it makes the sun jealous.

AUNT MAMA. What's dis doing out dere? *(Holding bucket.)* People be steal'n buckets. Some people piss like acid, burn right through day bucket. Make 'em steal.

She notices Isabel.

Hi, Miss Isabel.

ISABEL. What's all this fuss you making, Aunt Mama?

AUNT MAMA. Oh nuttin' much, ma'am. Jus dis little ole bucket, got me doin' dis big ole talkin'.

ISABEL. Keep that bucket outside.

Leaving it in here is why y'all smell so bad.

Listen to me.

I know.

I gotta smell ya every day.

I'm trynna help.

AUNT MAMA. I know, ma'am.

Isabel stares Mattie down.

ISABEL. Mattie, take that bucket from her and put it back outside.

Mattie takes the bucket from Aunt Mama and puts it back outside.

Look at that. Shit taking out shit.

She laughs.
Mattie reenters.

That scent of shit done came right back on in here. I gotta go. And remember, don't nobody sit in my chair. It's feeling a little funny.

Isabel leaves.
Silence.
Aunt Mama goes right to Isabel's chair and sits down.

AUNT MAMA. She uh evil bitch. Mattie get dat damn bucket and bring it back in here.

Mattie exits.
Again.

Mattie reenters.
Again.

What I tell you 'bout havin' her come in here and learnin' you?

MATTIE. You gonna get us all hanged, James.

AUNT MAMA. You know better. I spend all day out dere watchin' over all da planation's little ones 'fore day get old nuff ta know what it mean ta be us in dis evil whiteass world; shit, da last thing I wants is ta come in here and see her ole evil white ass. White people wear me out.

JAMES. What am I 'pose ta do?

I get hanged if somebody catch us.

Or I get hanged if I say no ta Miss Isabel.

I'm in a precarious predicament.

> *Precarious? They both look at James like he really is a learnin'*
> *boy.*
>
> *Beat.*

AUNT MAMA. Throw dat bucket uh acid piss in her face, and call it uh day.

> *They all laugh.*
> *Hard.*

JAMES. Aunt Mama, you so triflin'.

AUNT MAMA. I sho'll is. And you sho'll is uh learnin' one.

If you get hunged fa somefin',

Let it be cuz ya fight ta learn or fight fa freedom.

> *A moment.*

Freedom be good right 'bout now. Seem like since dat war done started day been extra evil ta us nowadays. Workin' us harder and whippin' us harder den dat. Like day trynna beat da thought uh freedom out us.

> *Beat.*

MATTIE. Look what I got!

> *Mattie pulls some bread from out her pockets.*

Massa Jacobs, and Miss Janie was too busy arguin' ta check me afta I leaves da kitchen.

So…

We gots us some good eats!

JAMES. Yea, we do!

Yea, we do!

AUNT MAMA. Come on here now. Let's sit at dis here table ta feast.

> *Mattie sits on the block.*
> *James gets cups and scoops water from out the other bucket.*
> *He passes the cups to Aunt Mama and Mattie.*
> *Since there is no other chair, he stands.*

But, he could care less. He 'bout to feast.
As they start to eat, the door flies open.
A man walks in.
He's tall, strong, and harder than the world that made him
this way; and he's dark—real dark.
His skin looks like the midnight hour—like something people
pray to.

Who you?

HENRY. Henry.

AUNT MAMA. What you doin' here?

HENRY. I come ta sleep.

MATTIE. Ain't no room in here fa no mo' niggahz.

AUNT MAMA. Quiet, Mattie.

HENRY. Da old man in da big house tells me ta come here. He tells me Aunt Mama da one dat teach niggahz how ta be on dis plantation.

AUNT MAMA. Dat's wat he tells ya?

MATTIE. Maybe he come here cuz it ain't dat many niggahz on dis planation, on account uh most uh 'em goin' off ta da war.

HENRY. Ain't you hear me just say dat old white man tells me ta come here and dat I comes ta sleep?

MATTIE. Just fa da night?

AUNT MAMA. Hush, gurl!

> *Beat.*
> *They all look at Henry.*
> *Then:*

Come on here ta dis table. We jus eatin'.

> *Henry walks up to the table.*
> *They never take their eyes off him.*
> *He stands next to James.*
> *Aunt Mama breaks some of her bread and gives it to Henry.*

HENRY. I lives here now.
I'm da new niggah.

Scene 3

Later that night.

James, Aunt Mama, and Mattie are lying in bed. Henry is lying on the floor.

Everyone is asleep—except Henry. While everyone else is in their undergarments, he's still in his clothes.

He's waiting to make his move.

After a few beats, he starts to make it.

He looks around to make sure everyone is asleep. When he realizes they are, he slowly gets up.

Sloooooooowly.

Even slower than that.
And be quiet.
We ain't trynna wake nobody!

He walks over to the table, takes the remaining bread and stuffs it in his pockets. Then he grabs a canteen and fills it with water.

He drinks.
All of it.

Then fills it up.
Again.

He takes a look out the window.
He takes a deeeeeep breath.
He's ready.

He starts to leave.

But,
He stops.

He hears dogs begin to bark in the distance.

He thinks…
He doesn't care.

This is his chance.

As soon as he gets one foot out the door:

AUNT MAMA. Ya heart maybe ready, but ya body ain't.

>*Henry stops.*

Ya tired.

Ya needs rest.

All da runnin' kind needs rest 'fore day run.

HENRY. I's rested up uhnuff.

>*Henry walks out on the porch.*

AUNT MAMA. You be dead 'fore da sun come up.

>*The barking gets closer.*
>*Henry stops.*
>*Aunt Mama goes out onto the porch.*

HENRY. Go back ta sleep.

AUNT MAMA. I neva was sleep. You ain't lemme do dat when you ain't take ya clothes off ta rest.

>*Beat.*

I was waitin' fa ya ta make ya move.

Since you is uh runnin' one.

HENRY. I gotsta get back ta ma family.

AUNT MAMA. We all gotsta get back ta our family.

And 'til we do,

We each otha family now.

HENRY. You…y'all ain't ma peoples.

>*Beat.*

AUNT MAMA. Da sky sure is extra pretty tanight.

Ain't it?

It's so dark. It look like our people's skin.

And dem stars—day so bright.

Make ya think dose we care 'bout most smilin' at us.

Right now.

HENRY. Dat's why I gotsta go.

Right now.

Da sky give me jus uhnuff light ta see,

and jus uhnuff dark not ta be seen.

AUNT MAMA. Who ya people is?

HENRY. *Ma* people.

AUNT MAMA. Da way you miss dem, I'm sure day miss you. Mighty much. But day is gonna miss you much more afta day find out you was hung'd—if day even do find out. Every man who eva lived in dis here shack was hung'd—'cept fa James. Dat's cuz he keep quiet. If he eva tries ta get his freedom he'll be smart uhbout it; he'll be quieter den da breeze at night, like I teach 'em. Like I can teach you, show ya uh different way den ya way. Da otha menz…day ain't wanna listen ta ma way. Day all tried ta do it da way you trynna do it right now. Ain't none of 'em make it.

HENRY. I will.

AUNT MAMA. You won't. Day watches dis shack in da late night. Step foot off dis porch and you uh dead man. You hear dem dogs barkin'. You know what dat mean…day searchin' fa runaways, and ya flesh be da sweetness day got uh taste fa. You be no good ta ya people dead. Come back in. Rest.

HENRY. 'Til I finds ma people I ain't gonna be able ta rest.

AUNT MAMA. Well, lay ya head down at least.
We can be ya peoples 'til you find da ones in ya heart.

HENRY. I said y'all niggahz ain't ma people.

Aunt Mama studies Henry.

AUNT MAMA. Why you say dat?

HENRY. Cuz y'all ain't!

AUNT MAMA. Nevamind dat. You gonna run ta us when ya meant ta run ta us. I'm talmbout why you say dat word? James and Mattie use it, too. *Why y'all call us nigger like day do?*

HENRY. We don't call us nigger.
We call us niggah?
We started dat ta take what day meant fa ugly,
ta turn it inta our beauty.

A moment.

AUNT MAMA. Why don't ya turn dis here inta ya beauty?

The dogs bark.
Henry just stands there…

Breathing.
Staring off into the sky.

Ya peoples…
Ya gots ta be smart 'bout how ya sees 'em uhgain…

A moment.

I bet ya peoples prolly lookin' up at da sky, too.
At its beauty.
Jus like you doing, right now.
Day right here.
Breathe 'em in.

Henry breathes.

Again.
And again.
And again.

Aunt Mama goes over to James.

(Loud whisper.) James! James! Wake up!

James, confused, begins to wake up.

JAMES. Huh?

AUNT MAMA. Come wit me.

JAMES. Wat's wrong?

AUNT MAMA. Jus come wit me, chile.

James gets up and follows Aunt Mama.

But stay ya ass right dere!
Don't come out on dis porch!
You know bettah.
If day see three us out here day bound ta hang us all.

James stops.
He sees Henry.

Staring at the sky.
And breathing.

Still.

Sing dat song da tree be hummin' in da wind.

James begins to hum.

23

It's a sweet, sweet tune.

Aunt Mama goes back into the shack, and gets in bed.

Henry continues to stare into the sky.

As James hums the sweet song that the tree taught him,

As the dogs bark in the near distance.

Scene 4

The next night.

James is in the shack—alone.

He's looking out the window—at the tree.

It's calling his name.

Mattie, Henry, and Aunt Mama enter.

Henry's nose is bleeding.

Mattie goes and dips a rag in the water bucket. She sits Henry on a bed, cocks his head back, and puts the rag on his nose.

Aunt Mama is hot about something.

AUNT MAMA. You don't talk ta no massa like dat!

HENRY. I talks ta 'em however I like.

AUNT MAMA. If ya wanna get hunged, yea ya do;
But if ya don't, den you don't give 'em no lip!

HENRY. I ain't gonna be here long.

AUNT MAMA. Cuz you gonna get hunged. Right out dere on dat tree.

HENRY. Ma neck ain't neva touchin' no noose!

AUNT MAMA. Keep it up and you gone be hangin' round dat tree jus like da otha ones.

JAMES. What you do?
What he do?

MATTIE. Massa Eugene was watchin' ova da fields. I comes ta give him some watah, since da sun was set on hell. As soon as I give him da watah, Henry stop pickin'; so Massa Eugene tell Henry keep pickin'. He tell Massa Eugene he need some watah. Massa Eugene say "You don't need no watah ya need ta work." Den he say, "All dis work ya got me doin' fa free, you gone give me some watah."

AUNT MAMA. He give dis fool uh blow ta da nose, wit his shotgun, is what he give 'em. I sees it all da way from da porch, wit da little ones.

JAMES. You always talks ta white menz like that?

AUNT MAMA. Don't go askin' him no questions.
Don't get ya head filled wit thoughts uh dis fool.

JAMES. I'm jus askin'. That's all.

AUNT MAMA. Don't ask dis fool shit!
Get back ta readin'.

MATTIE. Since Massa Jacobs and Miss Janie was arguin' uhgain, I gots ya uh new one!

> *Mattie pulls a newspaper from under her dress.*
> *She gives it to James.*

JAMES. Thank ya! I read the other one like fifty times. Front ta back.

> *James goes over to his bed to read.*
> *Aunt Mama goes over to Henry.*

AUNT MAMA. Let me take uh look at dat.

HENRY. I'm good.

AUNT MAMA. No ya ain't. Dat rag's 'bouts ta swim in ya blood.

HENRY. I said, I'm good.

AUNT MAMA. Ya don't gots ta be strong all da time.

HENRY. Yeah, I do.
Dat's how I survive.

AUNT MAMA. Ya don't gots ta be dat way here.
Not wit us.
Ya can show ya hurt.
Show it ta us.
Show it ta me.
Ya still strong if ya does.

> *Henry removes the rag from his nose.*

Mattie, get me ma work.

> *Mattie goes to a corner in the shack. She lifts a floorboard*

and pulls up a tiny drawstring bag.
She hands it to Aunt Mama.

Aunt Mama opens the bag. She takes a little of what's in the
bag and puts it in the palm of her hand.
It's…dust.
She puts the dust under Henry's nose.

Sniff.

HENRY. What's dat?

AUNT MAMA. Somefin' ta make ya feel betta.
Go on.
Sniff.

Henry hesitates.
He looks around—all eyes are on him.

Pause.

He sniffs.

He passes out.

Mattie girl, get me uh cup uh watah.

Mattie goes over to the water bucket and scoops water into
a cup.
She gives it to Aunt Mama.

Aunt Mama holds Henry's head and slowly gives him
some water.
He comes to and begins to drink.

Dat's it. Dat's right. Drink up.
Da ancestors in da watah.
Day'll make ya strong.

Henry sits up.

How ya feelin'?

HENRY. Betta.

AUNT MAMA. Like I knew'd ya would.

HENRY. What was dat?

AUNT MAMA. Somefin' dat makes ya feel betta when da struggle
gets too hard.

HENRY. What kinda woman you is?

AUNT MAMA. Uh old one, chile.
Prolly olda den God, lemme tell it.

>   *Beat.*

I sees da bleedin' done stop.

HENRY. Thank you.

AUNT MAMA. You ain't been here but one day.
I told ya, ya gots ta have smarts ta ya.
Not jus muscles.

HENRY. I gots ta get outta here.

AUNT MAMA. We all do, honey.

>   *Silence.*

JAMES. Look! Look!

>   *James holds up the paper.*

LOOK!

AUNT MAMA. You know ain't none uh us learnin' ones like you.

MATTIE. What? What it say?

AUNT MAMA. Read it.

JAMES. "There has been substantial talk of the state of America, in the White House—"

AUNT MAMA. I bet its nuttin' but us in dere, keepin' it runnin'.

MATTIE. Like always.
Call it da Niggah House.

JAMES. "President Abraham Lincoln has been going ta the State Capital ta meet with Congress."

MATTIE. What's Congress?

JAMES. That's…important people who meet up ta make things happen.

MATTIE. Oh.

JAMES. It say, "It's been speculated that within the next few months President Lincoln will be signing a bill…" and that's like, I think, uh law that ya gotta follow? It say, he'll be signing a bill "ta free all slaves."

MATTIE. Dat's what it really say?

JAMES. Yup! Right here.

AUNT MAMA. Ain't no such thing.

JAMES. Yeah, it is, Aunt Mama! It say it right here!

AUNT MAMA. All he gotta do is sign some papers?

JAMES. Yes, ma'am. It say it right here.

AUNT MAMA. And we all free?

JAMES. That's what this here paper say!

AUNT MAMA. Ain't no such thing!

MATTIE. We ain't gonna be free!

AUNT MAMA. Not dat easy at least.

JAMES. But dis paper say we is!

AUNT MAMA. Don't go believing everything you read. Specially if uh white man wrote it.

MATTIE. Day ain't gonna free us.

AUNT MAMA. We gonna have ta free ourselves.

James looks at the paper again with a dying hope.

JAMES. Y'all probably right.

AUNT MAMA. We is.

HENRY. Let me see dat.

Henry snatches the paper from James.
He looks at it.

AUNT MAMA. You uh learnin' one like he is?

HENRY. No.

AUNT MAMA. Den whatcha readin'?

HENRY. Dat we is gonna be free. I did ma share uh runnin'. I knows what's out dere in da world waitin' fa us. Freedom. If not from da war raging outside or from what dis here paper say or from us takin' it…one way or uhnotha we's gonna be free.

He slams the paper down.

We's gonna be free!

He starts to laugh a deep down kinda laugh.

Ha! Ha! We's gonna be free!!! Hahaha! We *is gonna* be free!!!! Hahaha!

They all stare at him.
Beat.

JAMES. We is gonna be free!

HENRY. Dat's right! Yea we is!

JAMES. We's gonna be free!

MATTIE. We's gonna be free?!

HENRY. Free! Free! Free! Free! Free!

AUNT MAMA. Stop wit all dis freedom talk!

      A hush falls over everyone, then:

Let's dance a freedom dance instead!

      Aunt Mama begins to Juba.
      James and Mattie join her.

      They all cheer, "We free!"

      Henry stands back and watches.

      As they dance their freedom dance.

Scene 5

The next day.

Sunday.

James and Henry are at the tree.

The branches majestically bend down and hide them—it's as if they're in the shack.

They're by the water.

The dogs are lightly barking, but that don't matter.

They're relaxing.

JAMES. I love the day uh the Sabbath.
No pickin', no runnin' errands, no nothin'.
We jus gets ta be.
I bet this what it feel like ta be white.
You eva wonder what's it like ta be white?

HENRY. No.

JAMES. Neva?

HENRY. Neva.

JAMES. Oh.

HENRY. I neva wanna be white.

JAMES. I ain't say nuttin' 'bout bein' white. I said wonderin'.

HENRY. I don't wonda kneever.
I loves da way my skin look.

JAMES. It is dark.

HENRY. Yeah.

JAMES. Like real dark.
Like "I can see myself in it" dark.

HENRY. Or God.
My mama usta always say, she can see God in ma skin.

JAMES. Yeah?

HENRY. Yeah.

JAMES. Where she at?
Where ya people?

> *Henry says nothing.*

I jus ask cuz, I was wonderin'. I ain't mean ta pry. You jus neva talk, and, well, you talkin'.

> *Henry still says nothing.*

We can talk about something else?

> *James tries to change the subject.*

This breeze from the watah feel real good.

> *Still—nothing; James tries again*

I hear this 'pose ta be one uh the hottest summers.

> *Silence.*

> *Henry just stares off into the sky.*

> *Then…*

> *He takes off his shoes and puts his feet in the water—still staring at the sky.*

He breathes.

So does James.
Silence and breaths.

HENRY. Iono.

JAMES. Huh?

HENRY. Ma people—iono where day at.

JAMES. You eva know?

HENRY. We all lived togetha in Georgia, but I ain't seen dem in months.

JAMES. What happened?

HENRY. We don't live togetha no mo'.

JAMES. Oh.

HENRY. We lived on uh nasty plantation, wit uh nasty white man.
So we runs.
But we get caught.
And 'stead uh hangin' us, day tear us 'part.
Dat feel worse den bein' hanged, I imagine.
Day say I ain't look like one uh dem war niggahz.
I think day just ain't wanna give me uh gun,
so day send me here ta work.
But as soon as dem papers get signed and I'm free, I'm findin' ma peoples.

The dogs bark.

JAMES. I'm sorry.

HENRY. You do it?

JAMES. Do what?

HENRY. Tear me 'part from ma mama, daddy, sister, and two lil brothas?

JAMES. No.

HENRY. Den what ya bein' sorry fa?

JAMES. I'm jus bein' benevolent towards ya. That's all.

HENRY. Ba-ne-vo-len?

31

JAMES. Compassionate.

Henry shoots him a look like, "Nigga, what?!"

Nice. I'm being nice toward ya.

HENRY. You really is uh learnin' niggah, huh?

JAMES. I guess I am.

HENRY. How ya learn so good?

JAMES. Miss Isabel.

HENRY. She da only child uh Jacob and Janie—right?

JAMES. Yeah.

You don't call 'em Massa and Miss?

HENRY. No.

JAMES. Why?

HENRY. I don't give no white person ma power no mo'.

Day think 'cause day spread ma family farer den day lies, all cross da South, dat day take ma power;

But day ain't.

Ma power jus gots a far reach now.

It's stronger den it eva was.

JAMES. It's true what you say ta Aunt Mama yesterday? 'Bout always bein' strong?

HENRY. Yeah—ain't no room in da world fa a weak niggah. It'll eat'cha alive.

JAMES. I ain't weak.

HENRY. I can tells dat. You mo' smart den strong, but ya still strong.

JAMES. I am.

HENRY. I wish I was boff, like you.

JAMES. I can teach you how ta be smart, if ya like.

HENRY. Ya could?

JAMES. I thinks. I try ta teach Mattie befo'. But she ain't neva really wanna learn. Say she be too tired from all the work they make her do in the big house. But, if ya want, I thinks I be good uh nuff ta teach you.

HENRY. How you know dat?

JAMES. Miss Isabel be done teach me fa ova uh year now. Say she wants ta be uh teacher. So, she been practicin' on me. Uh whole lot now since her husband, Massa William, go off ta fight in the war.

HENRY. You like her teachin' you?

JAMES. I like learnin'.

HENRY. You don't like her?

JAMES. I don't like how she look at me sometime when she teach me.

HENRY. How she look at ya?

JAMES. Like she lonely, like she sad. I sees it in her eyes e'vry time she look at me. Look like she wanna do more den teach.

> *Pause.*

HENRY. Like dis?

> *Henry demonstrates a look.*
> *It's more awkward than alluring.*

JAMES. More like this.

> *James demonstrates the look.*
> *It's dead on.*

HENRY. Dat's ugly.

JAMES. Yeah it is.

HENRY. Do it uhgain.

> *James does the look again.*
> *They both laugh.*

JAMES. This why I love the Sabbath Day.
We can jus be.
I like jus being.

HENRY. It do feel nice.
Undaneef dis tree and all.

> *Silence.*
> *They're just… Being.*
> *Then:*

Dis da biggest tree I done eva see.

JAMES. It go straight up ta heaven.

HENRY. Na, it don't.

JAMES. You see where it stop at?

HENRY. No.

JAMES. Cuz it stop when it touch da foot uh God.

HENRY. I should climb it!

JAMES. What?!

HENRY. I should climb dis tree.
Climb it all da way 'til I get ta God.
So I can ask him why we down here bein' treated like dis.

JAMES. Okay…but I ain't climbing that tree.

HENRY. You should!
Come on.
This way you's teachin' me how ta be smart.
And I's teachin' ya how ta be strong.

JAMES. I said no.

HENRY. Come on! Jus dis one time!

JAMES. Alright.
Come on.

HENRY. Henry da Muscles and James da Brain 'bout ta go on uh adventure ta heaven!

> They go over to the tree.
> They start to climb.
> They get pretty high.
> Then…
>
> The tree speaks.
> It's says, "Jamesssssss."
> James thinks nothing of it.
>
> But Henry is shocked.
> So shocked, he falls.
>
> James climbs down.
> He tends to Henry.

JAMES. You okay?

HENRY. You heard dat?
Dat tree talked!
It said ya name!
Dat tree said ya name!

JAMES. You heard it, too?!

HENRY. How could I not?
It scared da shit outta me.

>*A moment.*

JAMES. Me and Aunt Mama the only ones who know how special this tree is. Now you make three!

HENRY. Dis tree really talk?

JAMES. Yeah. It jus say ma name, but yeah. It talk.

HENRY. Dis some weird shit.

JAMES. No it ain't.
It's jus the ancestors talkin'.

HENRY. Why day call ya name?

>*Henry tries to get up.*

Ouch.

JAMES. No, no.
Stay down.
What hurt ya?

HENRY. Ma side.

>*James lifts Henry's shirt.*

JAMES. You got cut pretty bad.

HENRY. By da talkin' tree.

>*Henry takes off his shirt.*
>*James goes over to the water, takes his shirt off, wets it, and rubs it on Henry's wound.*
>*He sweetens it.*

You really is somefin' special.

JAMES. How this feel?

HENRY. Good.

JAMES. Good.

HENRY. What da tree call ya name fa?

>*A moment.*

JAMES. All the menz in ma life was hanged from the tree. Ma daddy was hanged from the tree. Shortly afta ma mama drowned in her tears from how bad her heartbreak. I don't got no people neither.

HENRY. You got Aunt Mama.

JAMES. She ain't ma aunt, or ma mama.
Not by blood, at least.
She jus so old she related ta e'body some kinda way.
Some say she was one uh the first slaves ova here.

> *Henry starts to sit up.*

Stay down.

HENRY. I'm okay.

JAMES. Ya better?

HENRY. Much.

JAMES. Yesterday ya gets ya nose bloody.
Today ya side.
Luckily ya gots me and Aunt Mama.

HENRY. Luckily.

> *Henry stares at James.*
> *James laughs.*

JAMES. You trynna be like Miss Isabel uhgain?

HENRY. No.

JAMES. Well, ya lookin' like her.

> *Silence.*
> *Then…*
> *Henry kisses James.*

What'cha… What'cha do that fa?

HENRY. Fa bein' sweet ta me.

JAMES. You kiss every man that's sweet ta ya?

HENRY. Jus you.

JAMES. Oh.

HENRY. Taday be's da first time I laughs, since bein' away from ma family.

JAMES. Well, I'm glad you laughin'.

HENRY. Me too. Dis da first time I gets ta jus…be.

The dogs bark in the distance.
A moment.
Henry kisses James again.

Scene 6

Later that night.

Everyone is in the shack, asleep.

Aunt Mama is on a bed.

Mattie is on a bed.

James is on a bed.

And Henry is still on the floor.

Everyone's sleeping peacefully, except Aunt Mama—she's snoring.

LOUD.

It's a surprise that the shack ain't shaking.

And except Mattie. She's up and restless.

She quietly gets out her bed and lies on the floor.

Next to Henry.

MATTIE. *(Whispering.)* Henry.
Henry.
You sleep?
HENRY. Not no mo'.
MATTIE. I thought ya mighta been up.
HENRY. Well, I wasn't.
Surprisingly.
It took me foreva ta block out Aunt Mama snorin'.
MATTIE. I'm sorry.
HENRY. What'cha want?
MATTIE. All her snorin'.
I's can't sleep.

HENRY. So ya wake me up?

MATTIE. Aunt Mama was gonna get ya soona or lata. I jus beat her ta it. Dat's all.

HENRY. True.
So,
What'cha want?

MATTIE. Ya know I usta live in da big house?

HENRY. No, I didn't.

MATTIE. I did.
When I was uh little girl,
I usta play wit Miss Isabel all da time.
But, some years uhgo, she started bein' real mean ta me, aftah Miss Janie had me kicked out…
Cuz Massa Jacobs tried ta sleep wit me.
Dat's why I got all deez wounds on ma face.
Miss Janie and Miss Isabel whip me real bad.
James found me down by dat tree,
almost dead.
He ain't know me dat well den,
on account uh me always bein' in da big house;
but he still brings me here ta Aunt Mama so she can do her work on me.
She said she surprise I's alive.
She ain't think dat dust she used on you would be dat powerful on me.

HENRY. Mighta been betta if you was gone.

MATTIE. Why ya say uh thing like dat ta me?

HENRY. Things prolly easier fa us in da aftalife.

MATTIE. Prolly is.

HENRY. See.
I ain't mean no harm by it.

MATTIE. Miss Isabel da one dat be da worse ta me.
I think it's cuz she uh curse woman—can't have no kids.
She take it out on me—by trynna whip me, trynna kill me.

    Beat.

If I was dead Massa Jacobs wouldn't still try ta sleep wit me. Ya wanna know why he stop right 'fore he gets inside me?

Silence.

Ya wanna?

HENRY. Why?

MATTIE. He ma daddy.

Beat.

He ain't tell me dat doe. Aunt Mama tell me. She say right afta my mama give birf ta me, day snatch me out her arms—and sold her off. Imma find her doe. When dem papers get signed, and I's free, I's gone find her.

Pause.

Ya got any family ya wanna find, when you gets free?

HENRY. Yea.

MATTIE. I guesses we all do.
We prolly all family anyway.
Da only family I got now, dat I knows of, is Aunt Mama.

HENRY. She old nuff ta be e'body kin.

MATTIE. She prolly really ma kin doe.
I thinks her and ma mama was sistahs.
Cuz sometimes, at night, Aunt Mama talk ta her in her sleep.
Dat's only when she not snorin' doe.

HENRY. Since livin' here in dis shack wit y'all, all I eva hear her do, at night, is snore.

Like clockwork, Aunt Mama snores.

MATTIE. Dat is da truth.
Her snorin' so loud it make me wanna go back and sleep in da big house sometimes.

HENRY. Make me wanna go ta da big house, too.

MATTIE. And if I go back ta da big house, maybe Massa Jacobs won't stop halfway. Maybe he go all da way wit me. I wouldn't mind.

Silence.

You think dat wrong since he not jus ma massa, but he ma daddy too?

Silence.

I been on dis earth mo' den twenty years and I's ain't neva have uh man inside me. Every man too scared ta touch me, cuz day know I's massa's daughta.

Silence.

You eva been inside uh girl before?

HENRY. Yes.

MATTIE. You like it?

HENRY. Yes.

MATTIE. You wanna be inside me?

Henry tries to find the words.

You can.

Still…no words.

I jus wanna be touched.

Touch ma thigh.

Please.

Henry touches her thigh.
Mattie takes his hand and drags it to her inner thigh.

Dat feel good.

Now.

Put it in me.

HENRY. I's tired, Mattie.

I gotta get uh good night sleep, so I can keep pickin' all da cotton I be pickin'.

MATTIE. Ya lips sayin' no, but dis ain't.

It keep growin' closa ta me.

It bridgin' dis space 'tween us.

Mattie throws herself onto Henry.

She moves her hips up and down, while she's on top of Henry.

Up and down.

She moves faster and faster.
They breathe harder and harder.

Until…

They stop.

They stare at each other.
That's all they can do.

Thank you.

Mattie gets up and goes back to her bed.

She isn't restless anymore.
In fact, she's sound asleep.

But not Henry.

He's up.

Scene 7

James is standing.
In front of the tree.
The branches are talking.
All of them.

BRANCH ONE. 1810–1850. Robert Lewis.

BRANCH TWO. 1789–1830. Charles Lewis.

BRANCH THREE. 1770–1791. Nathaniel Lewis.

BRANCH FOUR. 1752–1786. Jeffrey Lewis.

BRANCH FIVE. 1731–1770. George Lewis III.

BRANCH SIX. 1709–1751. George Lewis Jr.

BRANCH SEVEN. 1687–1740. George Lewis Sr.

BRANCH EIGHT. 1653–1692. Cesar Lewis.

BRANCH NINE. 1633–1679. Abel Lewis.

BRANCH TEN. 1600–1700. Abram Lewis. Formerly known as Mateku *("Ma-tee-koo.")* Egawn.

BRANCH ONE. James.

BRANCH TWO. James.

BRANCH THREE. James.

41

BRANCH FOUR. James.

BRANCH FIVE. James.

BRANCH SIX. James.

BRANCH SEVEN. James.

BRANCH EIGHT. James.

BRANCH NINE. James.

BRANCH TEN. Jamesssssssssssssssssss.

> *James just stands.*
>
> *And listens.*
>
> *As they introduce themselves.*
>
> *As they speak his name.*
>
> *All the while, he can't take his eyes off a particular branch.*
>
> *It's quite peculiar in the fact that it doesn't speak.*
>
> *It just grows.*

Scene 8

> *A few weeks later.*
>
> *Sunday afternoon.*
>
> *Aunt Mama and Mattie are in the shack.*
>
> *Mattie is doing Aunt Mama's hair.*
>
> *Aunt Mama looks like she's in pain.*

AUNT MAMA. Easy back dere, girl.
You know ma crown tenda.

MATTIE. I's almos done.

AUNT MAMA. You makin' dese braids so tight peoples gone be able ta reads ma thoughts. Massa Jacobs gone hang me fa what I's think 'bout him, fa sho'll.

> *Mattie laughs. Aunt Mama doesn't.*

I can't even laugh dese hurt so much.

42

MATTIE. I's almos done. Afta dis braid, jus uh few mo'.

AUNT MAMA. I hopes so.

>*Beat.*

MATTIE. Aunt Mama?

AUNT MAMA. Yes.

MATTIE. When you know'd you was uh woman?

AUNT MAMA. When I had ma first child.

MATTIE. Oh.
Dat was da only time you known?

AUNT MAMA. Yeah.

MATTIE. Oh.

AUNT MAMA. But I become uh woman one time, fa da first time, when uh red river run right down ma legs and I still don't stop pickin' cotton. Dats when I become uh woman.

MATTIE. Dere ain't no otha time ya know'd ya was uh woman?

AUNT MAMA. What ya fishin' fa, gurl?

MATTIE. I thinks I uh woman now.

AUNT MAMA. Cuz ya make love ta Henry, in da midnight hour, uh few weeks uhgo?

>*Pause.*

I only snore hard, not sleep hard.

MATTIE. He turned me into uh woman.

AUNT MAMA. Don't no menz turn ya into uh woman. You does dat on ya own.

MATTIE. He don't do dat wit me no mo' doe.
I try, but he don't.

AUNT MAMA. Maybe he ain't like what ya had ta give.

MATTIE. Dat happen ta you?

AUNT MAMA. Chile, all I gots ta gives now is dust.

MATTIE. Ya think I should stop tryin'?

AUNT MAMA. You think he wants ya ta keep tryin'?

MATTIE. No.

AUNT MAMA. Dere goes ya answer.

> *Silence.*
> *Just braiding.*

Whatcha think Love is?

MATTIE. Love?

AUNT MAMA. Yes. What's Love, pretty gurl?

MATTIE. Uh... Love is nice? It's, um, somefin' dat we feel. It's... *ma mama.* It's wat I feels when I think 'bout ma mama, when I feel like she thinkin' 'bout me, when I think she thinkin' 'bout me da same time I thinks 'bout her. It's you bein' ma mama, since I don't got one. It's you callin' me pretty even doe I gots all dese scars on ma face. It's bein' touched even when you got scars on ya face. It's smilin' brighta den da sun. It's wakin' up even when you don't know if ya gonna make it ta see da end uh da day. It's laughin' even when it seem like it ain't no joy nowhere round. It's findin' joy in somefin' as little as braidin' ya hair. Dat what Love feel like ta me.

AUNT MAMA. Dat sound like Love ta me, too. And Love don't have ta hurt. You may sometimes...uh lot uh times. But *it* don't have to. Now dese braids on da otha hand, dey hurt like hell!

> *The two laugh themselves into silence.*
> *More braiding.*
> *Until:*

MATTIE. All done.

AUNT MAMA. Thank ya, Mattie gurl.

> *Beat.*

MATTIE. Where dem boys at?

AUNT MAMA. Let 'em be.
Day be back up from da watah soon.

MATTIE. Well, I's thirsty.

AUNT MAMA. Let 'em be.
Day be back soon nuff.

> *Laughter is heard outside.*

And dere go soon nuff.

> *James enters.*

Henry follows. He handles a bucket full of water.

HENRY. I loves da Sabbath Day!
I jus gets ta be.

AUNT MAMA. Ain't nuttin' like it.

MATTIE. Give me dat bucket.

> *Mattie scurries over to Henry and takes the bucket from him.*
> *She proceeds to get herself something to drink.*

What took y'all so long?

> *James and Henry laugh.*
> *Still.*
> *Laughing.*

Well?

JAMES. Henry keeps climbin' that tree.
Keep thinkin' he can climb it ta heaven.

HENRY. I can.

JAMES. But he jus keep fallin'.

HENRY. I do.

JAMES. I keep havin' ta put 'em back together uhgain.

HENRY. He do.

JAMES. I sho'll do.

> *They laaaaaaaaaaaaaugh.*
>
> *It's magic in this laugh.*
>
> *So.*
> *Much.*
> *Magic.*
>
> *Aunt Mama even joins in.*
>
> *But Mattie…she just stares.*
>
> *She stares, and thinks.*
>
> *She thinks so loud that Aunt Mama hears her.*
>
> *She knows.*

AUNT MAMA. James, come wit me down ta da tree.

JAMES. We jus come from the tree.

45

AUNT MAMA. Well, come uhgain!
I gots ta get some new work from da roots.

HENRY. I can go.

AUNT MAMA. Naw, naw, naw.
Da real strong menz need ta rest on da Sabbath.

HENRY. Iono mind much.

AUNT MAMA. Naw.
Rest.
James, come on now.

> *Aunt Mama goes over to the corner, she moves the floorboard,
> gets her work, and exits.*
> *James follows right behind.*
>
> *Silence.*
>
> *Henry gets himself some water, and sits.*
> *On James' bed.*

MATTIE. You know he real *particular* like.

HENRY. Who?

MATTIE. James.
We gotta be out and workin' soon as da sun come up.
And his bed already made 'fore he even get outta it.

HENRY. Some menz is like dat, I guesses.

MATTIE. Some menz is. Real sweet like. Real...loathsome kinda
menz. Ya might wanna get up 'fore dat kinda *particular* jump on
ya.

HENRY. I's fine.

MATTIE. Well...
I don't wants ya messin' up his bed.
So...
Come sit ova here.
By me.

HENRY. I's comstable where I's at.
Plus, I's tired.

MATTIE. Ya always tired.

HENRY. Dis world always gives me reasons ta be.

Ma legs needs ta rest.
I's did fall out da tree.

MATTIE. Y'all always goin' down ta dat damn tree.
Fa da past two weeks—like e'day.

HENRY. We trynna get ta heaven.
Got some questions I need ta be askin' God.

MATTIE. I got some questions.

HENRY. We all got questions.
Da darka ya is, da more questions ya got.

> *Beat.*

MATTIE. Why don't ya like me, like I like you?

> *Beat.*

Like you like…

> *She can't say it.*
> *She can't even look at him.*
> *Beat.*

It be uh real shame if people eva find out da kinda particular James be.

> *The door opens.*
> *It's Isabel.*

ISABEL. James.

> *She looks around.*

Where James?

HENRY. Down by da tree.

ISABEL. He supposed ta be here.

HENRY. It's da Sabbath Day.
He free ta roam.

ISABEL. I know that, Henry.
What y'all in here doing?

HENRY. Restin'.

ISABEL. Resting?
You like *resting*.
Don't'cha, Henry?

HENRY. As much as da next menz, I guesses.

ISABEL. You probably got some *good* resting in you ta get out. Don't'cha, Henry?

> *Silence.*

Awe. Ya blushin'. I never seen somebody as dark as you blush.

> *Isabel walks over to Henry.*
> *Then…*
> *Something stops her.*

Why is this funkyass bucket still in here?
Didn't I tell you before to take, and KEEP, it outside, Mattie?

MATTIE. Yes, ma'am.

ISABEL. So why is it in here then?

MATTIE. People's steals buckets, ma'am.

ISABEL. What would somebody wanna steal a bucket for, Mattie?
That's 'bout the dumbest thing I done heard.
Go take that bucket outside.

> *Mattie gets up.*
> *She goes over to the bucket, to take it outside.*
>
> *She notices Henry.*
> *Henry notices her.*
>
> *Isabel notices them noticing each other.*
> *So…*
> *She stops Mattie.*

Give me the bucket.

> *Mattie gives Isabel the bucket.*
> *She smells it.*
> *She turns her nose up to it.*

Since ya skin already the color of piss, maybe you should smell like it too?

> *A moment.*
> *Then…*
> *She throws it in Mattie's face.*
>
> *Beat.*
>
> *Henry tries to comfort Mattie.*
> *Isabel notices.*

Beat.

You're never going to be white, Mattie. No matter how hard you try. You can never be like me. You can never be a sister. Never. We're nothing alike. Nothing.

A moment.

When James comes back tell him don't go leaving when I'm supposed to be teaching him. He doesn't know the type of trouble I could get in for learning him.

Beat.

And clean that up, Mattie.

Isabel exits.

Silence sits over the room.

Then…

Henry gets up.
He grabs a rag, dumps it in the water bucket, rings it out, and goes over to Mattie.
He begins to wash her face. Gently.
He's sweet on her.

MATTIE. Dis why I need ya on ma side.
Ma side.
Ma side.
Dis why, Henry.
Dis why.

Scene 9

The same day.
Maybe moments later.

James runs up to the tree.

Aunt Mama follows behind him.
Slowly.

JAMES. You so slow, Aunt Mama.

AUNT MAMA. I'm old.
Lemme catch up.

JAMES. Well, you caught up now.

AUNT MAMA. I is.

> *She just stares at the tree.*
>
> *So does James.*

JAMES. Uh few weeks uhgo I had ma first dream 'bout this tree.

AUNT MAMA. Did ya now?

JAMES. Yes, ma'am.

AUNT MAMA. What ya dream?

JAMES. That each branch had uh name.
They was people.
Ma people.
Ma daddy.
All the way up ta the first uh us ta get ova here.
His name was Mateku Egawn.

> *She smiles.*

AUNT MAMA. I dreams 'bout dis tree all da time.

JAMES. You do?

AUNT MAMA. I does.

JAMES. What you dream 'bout?

> *She smiles.*

AUNT MAMA. Ma people.
Ma chil'len.

JAMES. You was uh real mama once?

AUNT MAMA. Once?
Thirty-three times.

JAMES. Really?

AUNT MAMA. Yes, chile.
'Fore I was da one watchin' da babiez, I had ma own.
Day all dies off 'fore day come out me doe.
'Cept one.
Oshun what I name 'em.

I knows dat's uh girl name, but I jus love 'em so much.
He was as black as da midnight sky.
I saw all ma prayers answer'd in him.

> *A moment.*

He ain't live pass uh minute doe.
Soon as I hold 'em in ma arms,
And kiss 'em,
He go right back ta da one dat send 'em ta me.
I buried all ma babies round dis tree.

> *She just stares at the tree.*
> *So does James.*
> *Beat.*

JAMES. We jus come here ta stare at da tree?

AUNT MAMA. Nah, honey.
We comes ta get some uh dis tree's magic.
I need ya ta run round da tree 'bout three times.
Climb up it.
Grab a leaf.
Come back down.
Rip da leaf up.
Bury da leaf, unda da exact spot you got da leaf from.
And run round da tree 'bout three mo' times.
In da opposite direction.
Den kiss da tree.

JAMES. What?!

AUNT MAMA. Run round da tree 'bout three times.
Climb up it.
Grab a leaf.

JAMES. I heard ya. I jus can't believe ya.

AUNT MAMA. What you ain't believin'?

JAMES. That I gotta do all that.

AUNT MAMA. It's da ritual.
Da way it goes.
Now get.

> *James runs around the tree about three times.*

51

Climbs up it.

Grabs a leaf.

Comes back down.

Rips the leaf up.

Buries the leaf under the exact spot he got the leaf from.

And runs around the tree about three more times.

In the opposite direction.

Then he kisses the tree.

JAMES. Now what?

AUNT MAMA. We wait.

JAMES. Fa what?

AUNT MAMA. You'll see.

> *They wait.*
> *And wait.*
> *And wait.*

JAMES. How long we gonna wait?

AUNT MAMA. As long as we gots ta.

JAMES. The Sabbath gone be ova soon.

AUNT MAMA. Den we come back lata.

JAMES. Okay.

AUNT MAMA. You been comin' down ta dis here tree uh lot.

JAMES. I has?

AUNT MAMA. Don't act new.

JAMES. I has.

AUNT MAMA. What's dat 'bout?

JAMES. Well you knows the tree be talkin' ta me?

AUNT MAMA. I knows.
And I knows dat ain't da only reason you be comin' down here.

JAMES. It ain't?

AUNT MAMA. Don't act new.

JAMES. It ain't.

AUNT MAMA. You got uh smile ta ya, dat's different.

JAMES. I do?

AUNT MAMA. Yea.
What's dat 'bout?

JAMES. I jus be happy.

AUNT MAMA. Who?

JAMES. Who?

AUNT MAMA. Who put dat song in ya heart?

JAMES. Ya hear it?

AUNT MAMA. How can I not?
So.
Who?

JAMES. Who?

AUNT MAMA. Yea.
Who?

> *Beat.*

JAMES. How much longa we gotta wait?

AUNT MAMA. Not much longa.

> *Beat.*

You ain't jus uh learnin' boy.
You uh lovin' boy now.
Huh?

JAMES. Huh?

AUNT MAMA. Huh.

> *She smiles.*

Ya eva think Henry mean ta fall right 'fore he make it ta heaven?
Ya eva think he fall from heaven?
Dat he fall fa you?

JAMES. Huh?

AUNT MAMA. Huh.

> *She smiles.*

Da tree ain't even talkin'.
And ya still can't hear me doe?

But I's talkin'.
I's jus talkin' 'bout dat song in ya heart.
Jus talkin' 'bout love.
Jus talkin' 'bout…
Who.

JAMES. Who?

AUNT MAMA. Henry.

JAMES. *(Smiling.)* Henry?

AUNT MAMA. Yes'um, chile.
Ya fallin' angel.
Got'cha fallin' in ya feelin's.
Dat's who.

> *James is silent.*

Ya lips ain't talkin'.
But ya heart sho'll sangin'.
It sound…
Sweet.
Sound like…

BRANCH ONE. *(Singing.)* Love.

BRANCH TWO. *(Singing.)* Love.

BRANCH THREE. *(Singing.)* Love.

AUNT MAMA. And da wait is ova.

BRANCH FOUR. *(Singing.)* Love.

BRANCH FIVE. *(Singing.)* Love.

BRANCH SIX. *(Singing.)* Love.

JAMES. You hear that?

AUNT MAMA. How could I not?

JAMES. It ain't saying ma name no mo'.
It's sangin'.

AUNT MAMA. It sho'll is.

BRANCH SEVEN. *(Singing.)* Love.

BRANCH EIGHT. *(Singing.)* Love.

BRANCH NINE. *(Singing.)* Love.

AUNT MAMA. Don't e'body get dat typa song in day heart.

> *Beat.*

JAMES. Is this normal?

AUNT MAMA. What?
Love?
As normal as da sun rise in da mornin'.
As beautiful, too.

JAMES. I mean…

AUNT MAMA. What?
Say it.

> *James can't say it.*
> *He doesn't know how to.*

Dat song in ya heart…
Da one da tree taught ya…
Da one ya sung ta Henry da night he tried ta run…

JAMES. That song made him feel better that night.

AUNT MAMA. It sho'll did.
Love in dat song.

JAMES. Is me singing dat song to Henry normal?

> *Aunt Mama smiles.*

Me and Henry…
Is we normal?

AUNT MAMA. Yes, chile.
Y'all typa love go back ta Africa.
E'body lovin' e'body.
Menz lovin' menz.
Womenz lovin' womenz.
We ain't nuttin' but spirits, honey.
One spirit fall fa anotha spirit.
Don't care how da body look,
Jus care what da heart say.

JAMES. Really?

AUNT MAMA. Mhm.

JAMES. Ya eva feel this typa love before?

AUNT MAMA. Chile.

I's kiss da lips uh so many womenz.

And I ain't talkin' 'bout da ones on day face kneever.

JAMES. Aunt Mama!

AUNT MAMA. You ask'd!

> *Beat.*

JAMES. I'm okay ta be this way?

AUNT MAMA. Is dis way you?

JAMES. I guess.

AUNT MAMA. Den I *guesses* it is. I'm jus glad ya know who ya is.

JAMES. Did you know who I was?

AUNT MAMA. How could I not? It's uh beautiful thing ta know yaself.

> *A moment.*

But it's dangah ahead fa ya.

JAMES. What dat mean?

AUNT MAMA. Dat eh'thing ain't as good as it seem.

JAMES. Wit me and Henry?

> *Aunt Mama says nothing.*

How ya knows?

> *Aunt Mama reaches into her shirt.*
> *She pulls out a tiny bag that's attached to a thin string that*
> *hangs around her neck.*

AUNT MAMA. Dis here always stay close ta ma heart.

It's dirt,

from Africa.

Passed down ta me from all da womenz dat come 'fore me.

Dis keep me goin'.

Longa den I wanna be goin',

but it keep me.

It tell me things, too.

All typa things.

Not all things—jus all *typa things.*

Touch it.

> *James hesitates.*

Go on, touch it, boy.

James touches the bag.
Something happens.

He sees something.
He feels something.
All throughout his body.

He begins to tremble.

His trembles grow bigger,
and bigger,
and bigger.

Until...

He's eerily still.
Like he is frozen...

with sorrow.

All the while,
right after James touched the bag,
the tree has started to glow—and beat.

JAMES. That bag...it showed me hangin'.
It showed me hangin' from that there tree.

AUNT MAMA. Mhm.

JAMES. I's hangin' cuz uh Henry?

A moment.

AUNT MAMA. Wat's in dis bag be knowin' da things we don't.

JAMES. But I finally found ma song.
You tell me that.

AUNT MAMA. Dat don't matter.
Dat song may gots dangah in it.

JAMES. But it's ma song.
Dangah or not.
It's *ma* song.

James begins to weep.

Aunt Mama holds him.
She's sweet on him.

A moment.

You woulda been a good mama, Aunt Mama.

AUNT MAMA. I guesses I would.
Huh?

JAMES. Yes.

BRANCH TEN. *(Singing.)* Loooooooooove.

> *They listen to the tree…*

> *Beat.*

Scene 10

> *Dusk.*

> *A few days later.*

> *James and Henry are by the water.*
> *Hidden by the tree.*

> *They're very quiet.*
> *And very close.*

> *As if they're hiding something.*

> *In fact, they are.*

> *James is learning Henry.*

HENRY. "There. Has. Been. S…S…S… There. Has. Been. S…S…S…
There. Has. Been. S…S…S…"

JAMES. *(Annoyed.)* Substantial! "There has been substantial talk of
the state of America, in the White House!"

HENRY. Oh.

JAMES. Try uhagain.

HENRY. "There has been sssssub-stan-tial talk of the sssssstate of
Ah…ah…ah…"

JAMES. Sound it out.

HENRY. Ah…ah…

JAMES. I'll help.

58

HENRY and JAMES. Ah-mer-ric-ca.

HENRY. Ah-mer-ric-ca.

JAMES. Read it uhgain.

HENRY. "There has been sssssub-stan-tial talk of the state of Ah…ah…ah…"

JAMES. America! The word is America!

HENRY. I'm sorry. I's tryin'.

JAMES. This the only paper we read. We read this part like a hundred times. You should know it by now.

HENRY. I really is tryin'.

JAMES. Let's jus stop. We done fa the day.

HENRY. Okay.
You okay?

JAMES. I'm fine.

HENRY. *(Like: you lyin'.)* Niggah.

JAMES. I is.

HENRY. Aunt Mama gave me some herbs. Said it's good ta smoke when ya need uh calmin'. Want some?

JAMES. Nah. I don't mess wit' that.

HENRY. Ya wanna climb da tree den?

JAMES. Nah.

HENRY. Cuz ya tired?

JAMES. I guesses you can say that.

> *Henry looks around,*
> *to make sure the coast is clear.*
>
> *It is.*
>
> *So…*
> *Henry starts kissing James' neck.*

I said I's tired, Henry.

HENRY. I'll give ya uh reason ta be tired alright. Dese branches hidin' us from da world so I can get down ta business.

> *Henry continues to kiss up on James.*

JAMES. I's real tired Henry.

HENRY. Ya did run uh lotta errands and do uh lotta pickin' taday.
I guess me teachin' ya how ta be strong workin'.
I sees ya muscles gettin' all big.

JAMES. I guesses day is.

> *Henry's still kissing James.*

Stop.

> *Still kissing.*

I said stop!

> *Beat.*

Why you like me the way you do?

HENRY. Whatcha mean?

JAMES. I ain't neva been wit no man befo'.

HENRY. Me kneeva.

JAMES. But you been wit womenz befo'. Not me. I ain't neva been wit
nobody. Not eva. Da first time we made love was da first time I eva
seen a naked body otha den ma own. Ya saw how scared I was…every
single time ya touched me, every time ya kissed me. I kept wonderin'
why me? Every single time I asked myself dat question. So…why me?

> *Henry says nothing.*

You back ta bein' quiet now? Huh?!

> *Henry says nothing.*

Say somefin', Henry!
Why you like me the way you do?!
This loathsome way.
This way that got Mattie bein' worse ta me than the ones in the big
house, cuz you don't like her this way.
So why me?!

HENRY. Cuz I feel like I can get closa ta God wit ya!
Dat's why we be climbin' dis tree—right?!

> *Beat.*

And I don't miss ma family, as bad, when imma round you.

> *A moment.*

How long ya wanted ta ask me dis?

> *James says nothing.*

Dis why you been actin' da way ya been actin' da past few days...
Why you been walkin' round like somebody stole ya smile...
Dis why you been hummin' dat sad song lately?

> *A moment.*

I smile when imma round you.
I laughs when imma round you.
When imma round you I jus gets ta be.
If dat ain't what ya want, lemme know now.
Free me from you,
so I can go back ta findin' ma people.
If ya jus tell me ta go I go.
Go on and free me,
if dat's wat ya want.

> *A moment.*

Well, I'll free myself then.
Jus know I was scared too.
But my Love is stronga den ma fear.

> *Henry begins to leave.*

> *Beat.*

Come on, James.
Please.
It's getting dark.

JAMES. Don't you go worryin' 'bout me.
Go on.
I'll be comin'.
Me and this tree jus gots some talkin' ta do first.

> *A moment.*

> *James smiles a sad smile to Henry.*

> *Henry catches it,*
> *and gives it back,*
> *then leaves James there...*

> *With the tree.*

And the state of him and Henry.

Scene 11

Day.
A couple days later.
Henry is by himself.
Trying to climb the tree.
Still.
He gets pretty high up.
Then…
He falls—from the same spot, as always.
He gets back up and begins to climb again.
Isabel walks up.
She sees him.

ISABEL. Henry!
If you don't get down!
Get.
Down.

   Henry gets down.

That was so dangerous.
You could've hurt yourself.
Are you okay?

HENRY. Yes.

ISABEL. I don't want to see you climbing this thing again.
Niggers don't climb trees, they get hung from 'em.
I don't know why my daddy don't cut this one down.
It's so big and ugly to look at.
Ain't it?

HENRY. No.

   Pause.

ISABEL. Well, I guess niggers gotta get hung somewhere.

> *Beat.*

I've been looking for you.
They said I'd find you down here, by this tree…
Climbing it.
Is that how you get your muscles?

> *She feels on Henry's biceps.*

HENRY. No.

ISABEL. Then how?
It's so…
Big.

HENRY. *(Straight face.)* Pickin' cotton.

ISABEL. We needs to have you pick cotton round the clock then.
Don't we?

> *Silence.*

Should we have you pick cotton round the clock?

HENRY. *(Straight face.)* No.

ISABEL. I guess you're right.
How else you gonna find time to *rest*?
With me.

> *Silence.*

If that piss girl wasn't in the shack the other day, would you have *rested* with me?

> *Silence.*

I'm talking to you now. It's polite to talk back.
Would you have rested with me?

HENRY. *(Straighter face.)* No.

> *Pause.*

ISABEL. 'Cause you scared?
'Cause I'm white and you a nigger?
Don't be scared.
It's okay.
My husband been off for the past six months fighting in that war.
And might be gone for another six.

He ain't never gonna know.

Come on.

You know you want to.

I want you to...

  Beat.

I haven't been touched the way in which a woman needs to be touched in so long...

  Isabel moves her hand from Henry's bicep, across his chest,
  down his stomach, and rests it on his crotch.

This so big, too.

  She starts massaging it.

It's getting bigger.

  She puts her hand inside his pants.

Wow.

You aren't scared at all.

What you want to do with this big ole thang?

  Silence.

I know what you can do with it.

  She's still massaging it.

Come lay me down behind this tree.

  Henry. Is. Still.

I said come on!

HENRY. No!

  She stops massaging.
  She squeezes him.

  Pain.

  Henry pushes Isabel.
  She falls to the ground.

  Embarrassed.

ISABEL. You's a stupid nigger!

A stupid, stupid nigger!

  Henry runs.

You ain't gone be able to get far!

This tree got a branch with your name on it, Henry!
You hear me!
You's a dead nigger now!

> *Henry's gone.*

Scene 12

> *The same day.*
> *Moments later.*
>
> *James is sitting on his bed...*
> *Humming a sad song.*
>
> *Henry busts in.*
>
> *He notices James.*
>
> *Beat.*
>
> *He runs to the table, grabs some bread crumbs, and stuffs them in his pocket.*
>
> *Then he gets a canteen and fills it with water.*
>
> *He goes to exit.*
>
> *Before he does,*
> *James stops humming and says:*

JAMES. I can learn ya one mo' time 'fore ya go.
I only got this same ole paper though,
since Mattie don't neva bring me no new ones no mo'.
Jus threats uh tellin' massa I know how ta read.
Jus grief.
But I can still learn ya, in ma grief, 'fore ya go...
if ya like.
HENRY. Naw.
I gots ta be goin' now.
JAMES. Where?
HENRY. Iono.
But I jus gots ta get outta here.

JAMES. Cuz uh us?

HENRY. Naw.
Cuz I push Isabel.
I push her hard on da ground.

JAMES. Why you do uh dumb thing like that?

HENRY. She try ta lay down wit me.

JAMES. Oh.

HENRY. But I ain't do it doe.
I push her down.
And she scream, "You dead nigger."

JAMES. So ya really do gots ta go…and be the runnin' niggah ya is.

HENRY. Yea.
I does.

     Beat.

JAMES. But maybe not.

HENRY. Why?

JAMES. This here paper.
Memba?
It say we gonna be free.
They can't hang you cuz we gonna be free.

HENRY. We ain't free yet, so day can do whateva day want.
I gots ta go.

JAMES. But…
Don't.
Please.

HENRY. I gots ta.

     Beat.

Come wit me.

JAMES. What?

HENRY. Come wit me.
We can run off tagetha.
Start uh new life.
Jus me and you.
We can jump ova da broom, too.

If day freein' slaves, I'm sho'll day let us jump into faeva wit each otha.
What ya say?

> *James looks at Henry.*

> *As if he sees a home in him.*
> *As if he sees a life with him.*

> *It looks...*

> *Sweet.*

Ya gotta tell me now, James.

> *A moment.*

JAMES. I can't.

HENRY. What?

JAMES. I.
Can't.

HENRY. Why?

JAMES. I can't end up like the otha menz in ma family.
I can't run.
It's dangah ahead fa us if I do.

> *Beat.*

We can't be tagetha.
Not right now at least.

> *The two can't look at each other, because they know what*
> *comes next.*

HENRY. I gots ta go.

> *Henry kisses James.*

> *His hardness starts to break.*

JAMES. I love you.

HENRY. I love you, too.

> *They kiss again.*

> *There's a noise coming from outside.*

Dat's dem.
Day comin' fa me.
I gotta go!

Henry begins to run off.

JAMES. Imma meet ya!
I don't know when, but I will.
Ma heart and yours got the same song, so imma find ya.

They kiss.

One.
More.
Time.

Dogs begin to bark.

Henry runs to the door. It opens.

It's Aunt Mama.

Henry runs into her as he's trying to escape.

AUNT MAMA. What ya movin' so fast fa?
Ya trynna knock me ta ma grave?

HENRY. No.
Day trynna kill me.

AUNT MAMA. Who?

HENRY. Isabel.

AUNT MAMA. Why?

HENRY. I push her down.
Then she say she gonna hang me.

AUNT MAMA. Chile.

HENRY. So I gots ta go!

JAMES. Tell 'em he don't gots ta, Aunt Mama.
Tell 'em.
Please.

Silence.

AUNT MAMA. I can't do no such uh thing.

The door flies open.
It's Mattie.
She's out of breath.

MATTIE. Run!

HENRY. I is.

MATTIE. Day comin' fa ya!

When I was in da big house, Miss Isabel come runnin' in—cryin'.

All I hear her say is you rape her, and I come runnin'!

Cuz dat look in Massa Jacob's eyez was sayin', "It's time ta hang uh nigger."

Run!

HENRY. I is.

> *The dogs grow louder.*

> *Beat.*

> *Henry hugs them all.*

> *James rushes over to Aunt Mama's corner; he removes the floorboard, grabs Aunt Mama's bag, and pours some of the dust in Henry's hand.*

JAMES. Use this when ya out there.

When ya get hurt, rub it on ya wounds.

The sweetness of it will make ya feel better.

Keep ya strong.

Just like our song.

Listen ta the tree.

It'll tell ya what ta do.

HENRY. I will.

> *Henry's gone.*

JAMES. It'll tell 'em what ta do—right, Aunt Mama?!

It'll tell 'em.

It'll tell 'em.

He'll be fine.

He'll be real fine.

The tree'll tell 'em what ta do.

We'll be togetha uhgain real soon.

Scene 13

A few months later.

Night.

Aunt Mama and Mattie are sitting at the table—eating.

More than bread.

More so Aunt Mama.

Mattie really isn't touching her food.

If it weren't for the dogs barking in the distance it would be quiet.

Real quiet.

Mattie begins to moan.

AUNT MAMA. Da sickness still got ya?

MATTIE. Yes, Lord, it does.

AUNT MAMA. Go lay down.
Rest.

MATTIE. I can't even hold no food down no mo'.

AUNT MAMA. Dat's how it be's sometimes. Was wit me.
Da sickness'll pass.

MATTIE. You said dat months uhgo.

AUNT MAMA. It will. Jus trust.
Lay down now.
Get undaneef dat blanket and rest, honey.

> *Mattie gets up from the table.*
>
> *Her stomach is big.*
>
> *Real.*
>
> *Big.*

Ya stomach drops pretty low. Ya may have ya uh boy.

MATTIE. I jus may.

> *Mattie goes and lies down.*
> *Aunt Mama is still at the table—singing.*

AUNT MAMA.

> *Deep down in ma heart,*
> *I gots uh song so big*
>
> *Deep down in ma heart,*
> *I gots uh song so big*
>
> *Deep down in ma heart,*
> *I gots uh song so big*
>
> *It go love*
> *It go love*
> *It go love*

MATTIE. Where ya hear dat song from?

AUNT MAMA. Da wind.

MATTIE. I like dat song.

AUNT MAMA. Me too.

MATTIE. Can ya sing it uhgain?
It drown out dem damn dogz.

AUNT MAMA. Day iz louda den usual tanight.

> *Aunt Mama walks over to Mattie, sits on her bed, rests Mattie's head in her lap, as she rubs her hair and sings.*

> *Deep down in ma heart,*
> *I gots uh song so big*
>
> *Deep down in ma heart,*
> *I gots uh song so big*
>
> *Deep down in ma heart,*
> *I gots uh song so big*
>
> *It go love*
> *It go love*
> *It go love*

MATTIE. Thank you. You sangin' dat make ma sickness light.

AUNT MAMA. You wouldn't even know'd ya ailin' from how good ya be doin' wit all da extra work Miss Janie and Miss Isabel be givin' ya in da big house.

MATTIE. Bein' uh niggah don't stop when life get too hard fa ya.

AUNT MAMA. Ain't dat da truth.

71

MATTIE. And I can do da work real easylike cuz I puts uh little pee in day soup every evenin'.

> *A moment.*

> *They burst with laughter.*

AUNT MAMA. You sho'll is nasty.

MATTIE. I sho'll is.

> *Aunt Mama hums the song from the wind.*

> *Then...*

> *The door opens.*

> *It's Henry.*

AUNT MAMA. Henry?!

HENRY. Yeah.

AUNT MAMA. What you doin' here?

HENRY. I comes back.

AUNT MAMA. I sees dat... Ya still gots da dust?

HENRY. Uh little bit.

AUNT MAMA. Good. You been survivin' out dere?

HENRY. Barely. It's real bad out dere. And so cold. I hardly rested any. Wheneva I was able ta close ma eyes it was wit da sounds uh gunshots, bombs, and screams. Day da sounds dat wake me up, too. And you don't know where it's comin' from. It's jus nuttin' but space unfoldin' into mo' space out dere. I can't tell da East, from da West, from North, from da South. And da North Star ain't as bright as day say.

AUNT MAMA. I guesses it ain't, if ya back here.
Dis deep down South.

> *Dogs bark.*

Ya know ya can't stay here.

HENRY. I knows.
I's jus gonna rest ma eyes fa uh little bit.
I leaves 'fore da sun wakes up.

> *Pause.*

Hi, Mattie.

MATTIE. Hi, Henry.

Mattie starts to get up.

AUNT MAMA. Stay down.

MATTIE. I's can get up.
Give 'em uh hug at least.

> *Mattie gets up.*
> *Henry notices her stomach.*
> *They hug.*
> *It's long.*
> *Beat.*

HENRY. Dat's mine?

MATTIE. Yes.

HENRY. I's gonna be uh daddy, huh?

AUNT MAMA. Yes you is.

HENRY. Make sho'll it know who I is.

MATTIE. I will.
He will.

HENRY. He?

MATTIE. Yes, he.

> *Henry smiles.*

Imma teach him wat I know.
How ta be strong, wat love is.
Aunt Mama gonna help me raise him.

AUNT MAMA. Massa Jacobs thinks it's his.
He keep feedin' Mattie real good cuz uh it.

> *Henry looks at the table—hungrily.*

HENRY. I sees.

AUNT MAMA. When da last time ya ate?

HENRY. Long uhgo.

AUNT MAMA. Come on and sit on down.
Get ya some eats.

> *Henry goes over and sits at the table.*
> *He makes himself a plate.*
> *He eatsssssss.*

This is probably his first meal in days—maybe even weeks.

You can take some witcha when ya go.
We get so much; and Mattie hardly eat any of it—
wit her sickness and all.

HENRY. Thank you.

> *Aunt Mama and Mattie watch Henry eat.*
>
> *Then look at each other.*
>
> *Henry notices.*

Dis real gud.

AUNT MAMA. We sees.

> *Beat.*

HENRY. Where James?
He at da tree?

AUNT MAMA. Yea.

HENRY. He loves him dat tree.

AUNT MAMA. James and dat tree is one.

> *Dogs bark.*

Day sound like day gettin' closa.

HENRY. I won't bring 'em ta ya doorstep.
I promise.
Afta I see James I'll go.

MATTIE. Where you gonna go?

HENRY. Iono.
I don't gots nowhere ta go.

AUNT MAMA. You gots ya peoples.

HENRY. Naw. I spent faeva trynna find dem, and I come up empty-handed. 'Til I come here. Y'all ma peoples.

AUNT MAMA. You always been our people.
It took ya awhile, but ya found ya way ta us.

> *The dogs bark.*

HENRY. You said James be back soon, right?

AUNT MAMA. I said, him and dat tree one.

HENRY. Well, he needs ta leave dat tree uhlone and come back here 'fore I's leaves. He can try ta climb up ta heaven lata.

MATTIE. He ain't gotta do much tryin'.

HENRY. What dat mean?

> *Aunt Mama and Mattie don't say anything. They just look at each other.*
> *Henry notices.*

Huh?

AUNT MAMA. Boy, give da food uh chance ta catch up ta ya stomach.

> *Henry stops eating.*
> *Beat.*

HENRY. What dat mean?

AUNT MAMA. Dat ya needs ta slow down.
Ya eatin' too fast.

HENRY. No—what dat mean, 'bout James and da tree?

> *A moment.*

AUNT MAMA. Afta ya left James don't be James no mo'...

MATTIE. He get real sad; and dat sad song he was singin' befo' ya left get sadda...

AUNT MAMA. Da tree even join in and start singin' dat broken-hearted song wit 'em. From sun up, ta sun down, ta sun up uhgain. Him and dat tree was jus cryin' out...

MATTIE. It was da saddest thing ya done eva heard...

> *A moment.*

AUNT MAMA. I tries ta talk some sense inta 'em...
Get 'em back in his right mind...
But it was nothin' ta be done...
He was gone...

MATTIE. No mo' talkin'...
No mo' readin'...
Jus dat song...

AUNT MAMA. Uh few times he tried ta run—like you...

MATTIE. Prolly ta you...

75

But we stop him…
Calm him down…

AUNT MAMA. But dis one day he jus be so sad, he snap…

MATTIE. He go crazy…

AUNT MAMA. He stop pickin' cotton and he runs down ta dat tree…
He climbs up it, like he trynna get ta God…
But when he gets ta dis one spot…

MATTIE. Da spot ya always fall from…

AUNT MAMA. He start cryin' out ta God…
Cryin' out ta you…

MATTIE. Wailin'…

AUNT MAMA. "HENRY!"

MATTIE. Dat's when me and Aunt Mama runs ta 'em…

AUNT MAMA. We tries one mo' time ta talk some sense inta 'em…

MATTIE. We tries ta get 'em ta come down from da tree, cuz we
sees massa comin'…

AUNT MAMA. But he don't come down… He jus keep wailin'
'bout you…

MATTIE. 'Bout how much he miss ya…
How much he wanna hold ya…
How much he wanna kiss ya…

AUNT MAMA. Eh'body hears it…

MATTIE. Even Massa Jacobs…

AUNT MAMA. And eh'body get it…

MATTIE. The kinda *particular* he is…

AUNT MAMA. Even Massa Jacobs…
So…
he hunged 'em.

A moment.

HENRY. Dat's why he ain't neva meet me?

AUNT MAMA. Dat's why.

HENRY. How it happen?
Exactly.

76

AUNT MAMA. Ya sure ya wants ta know?

HENRY. Yes.

AUNT MAMA. Massa Jacobs go crazy...

MATTIE. Real crazy...

AUNT MAMA. He keep screamin', "We gots loathsome nigger boys fuckin' loathsome nigger boys on dis plantation."

MATTIE. Crazy...

AUNT MAMA. He hurt James...

MATTIE. Bad...

AUNT MAMA. 'Fore day hunged him on dat tree, day whips 'em...

MATTIE. Bad...

AUNT MAMA. Give 'em wounds dat open wider den his heart fa you. Den massa pour sugar....

MATTIE. In da wounds.

AUNT MAMA. Make all da air smell sweet from his insides...

Henry begins to weep.

You want me ta stop?

MATTIE. She can stop...

AUNT MAMA. I's stop...

MATTIE. Stop.

HENRY. Keep goin'.

AUNT MAMA. Massa Jacobs cut his manhood off right 'fore he hunged 'em...

HENRY. He was in pain?

AUNT MAMA. He ain't neva say uh mumblin' word...

MATTIE. 'Cept, "Tell Henry I love 'em."

AUNT MAMA. Dat's all he say...

MATTIE. And dat's when I really gets it...
When I know what y'all had...
I know why ya usta look at him da way ya did,
when he wasn't even lookin' ya way...

AUNT MAMA. Love...

MATTIE. "Tell Henry I love 'em."

AUNT MAMA. Dat's all he say…
He was quieter den da breeze at night…

HENRY. When dis happen?

AUNT MAMA. Last week.

> *A moment.*

HENRY. He was 'pose ta meet me.
We was 'pose ta find each otha.
I comes back so we could be tagetha uhgain.
Befo' I leaves he say we couldn't be tagetha right den,
But I gives it some time,
like he say we need,
so we can be tagetha now.
I wanted ta come back soona,
but I got lost.
I couldn't find ma way.
Night afta night I tried ta find ma way back ta him, but I couldn't.
I couldn't.
Den I hear it.
Da tree start talkin'.
Callin' ma name.
Its voice lead me back here.
But James ain't here.
He ain't here.
And I want 'em here.

> *Henry goes over to Aunt Mama's corner; he removes the floorboard, grabs the bag, and gives it to her.*

Bring 'em back!

AUNT MAMA. I can't.

HENRY. Yea ya can, old woman!
Use ya magic.
Dis'll bring 'em back.

MATTIE. Dere ain't no body.

HENRY. Why?

MATTIE. Afta day hung 'em, day feed 'em…

>*Dogs bark.*

Ta da dogs.

AUNT MAMA. I couldn't bring 'em back even if I wanted ta.

HENRY. But I want 'em here.
Wit. Me.
Our hearts gots uh song dat day sing togetha.
We was gonna have uh faeva tagetha.
Dats wat we used ta talk 'bout.

AUNT MAMA. I know, baby. I know. But I need you ta know dat da past and da future, everything dat was and everything dat's gonna be, always folds inta each otha ta give us right now. Dis moment. Find da love dat's in *dis* moment.

HENRY. *(Defeated.)* I can't.

AUNT MAMA. Yea ya can. Memba how ya said ya turn ugly inta beauty. Turn dis ugly inta ya beauty.

HENRY. How?

AUNT MAMA. Breathe.

>*Henry breathes.*

>*Still.*

Dat's it. Dat's right.
Now feel 'em.
He is here.
James is right here.

>*She points to his heart; she points out.*

Breathe 'em.
He right in dat dere tree.
Look. You'll see 'em.

>*They all go by the window and look at the tree.*

>*Aunt Mama on one side of Henry; Mattie on the other.*

>*Henry is no longer the hard man that we first met.*
>*He breaks completely down.*

>*They lift him*
>*Up.*

HENRY. I don't see 'em!

AUNT MAMA. Look harder.
He dere.

> *Henry looks harder.*
>
> *He sees something.*
>
> *They all do.*
>
> *It's a branch, skinnier than the rest.*
>
> *It grows, from out the tree.*
>
> *It keeps growing.*
>
> *And growing.*
>
> *And growing.*
>
> *And growing.*
>
> *All the way up.*
>
> *And Henry hears something.*
>
> *It's the tree.*
>
> *It beats.*
> *Beats.*
> *Beats.*
>
> *Like a heart.*
>
> *The dogs continue to bark,*
> *but they get drowned out.*
>
> *By the heartbeats*
> *And by the humming.*
>
> *The humming in the air.*
> *It sounds…*
>
> *Sweet.*

End of Play

PROPERTY LIST
(Use this space to create props lists for your production)

SOUND EFFECTS
(Use this space to create sound effects lists for your production)

Note on Songs/Recordings, Images, or Other Production Design Elements

Be advised that Dramatists Play Service, Inc., neither holds the rights to nor grants permission to use any songs, recordings, images, or other design elements mentioned in the play. It is the responsibility of the producing theater/organization to obtain permission of the copyright owner(s) for any such use. Additional royalty fees may apply for the right to use copyrighted materials.

For any songs/recordings, images, or other design elements mentioned in the play, works in the public domain may be substituted. It is the producing theater/organization's responsibility to ensure the substituted work is indeed in the public domain. Dramatists Play Service, Inc., cannot advise as to whether or not a song/arrangement/recording, image, or other design element is in the public domain.